Our Hummingbird Friends
Coloring Book
By Joe L. Blevins

ISBN-13: 978-1537605739

ISBN-10: 1537605739

To Camryn and Carrigan.

Color these birds and cut them out to put on the colored backgrounds, that don't have any hummingbirds. A few drops of glue smeared on the back will keep them as you want them. I hope that you enjoyed them as much as I did drawing them for you. Thank you!

Color with a friend!

Read together and celebrate each day!

Books by Joe L. Blevins LLC.
© 2016-09-09

Books by Joe Blevins LLC.

Search www.amazon.com

Find : BOOKS

Then see : joe blevins

www.hattrick2014.jb@gmail.com

ISBN-13:
978-1537605739
ISBN-10:
1537605739

About the Author

Joe L. Blevins is an author of over fifteen years and an illustrator for over forty years. Blevins' books range from horror, historical, and more family oriented tales. Joe's stories always use an element of history as a base for the premise. Joe uses life events and details to let his stories ring true to the reader. Most of all: reading is to be fun and informative for all ages. Joe worked for twenty-six years in electronics, and twelve years as a teacher at three different school districts. While he acted as a teacher he was involved in various reading programs. There he saw a need to make better stories for young readers. He saw what the students liked and what they did not. This was his real "education" as an author by learning that readers demand more than just a good story. They need something that "speaks" to them as a person. These are books that the reader can actually relate to. Blevins worked with many students with learning disabilities. He also worked with some hearing impaired students. These students needed a story tailored for their needs with brightly colored illustrations to keep the reader interested. Joe continues to write some new books: Pixie Land, Double Trouble and Domino Makes New Friends. Blevins writes for children and those that love to read to them. Now Mr. Joe Blevins has teamed up with Madame Louise Lamontague for some new books translated into French language versions: Deux fois les ennuis,(Double Trouble) Colton le cowboy,(Cowboy Colton) and Les Comptines de Gaston's,(Doonce's Nursery Rhymes.) Joe invites you to read his stories and make comments, if you wish. Thank you.